Minecraft: Diary of A Minecraft Steve Trapped in Minecraft

BOOK 1

Table of Contents

Steve Meets Alex

Chapter 1: An Unexpected Visitor Arrives

Our story begins where all stories do. Something strange and mysterious is about to happen to an ordinary person. Steve had been working hard to build a home in the new world in which he found himself. He was trying to survive the attacks of zombies, skeleton archers and worst of all, the explosive creeper. Where our story meets him, he has been out in the forest collecting wood, cobblestones and dirt for his house, as well as food for himself when he noticed that night had suddenly crept upon him. Steve packed up his finds and headed home. As he approached his house he noticed somebody standing in the shadows near it, creeping around. Not wanting to be seen by the unknown visitor, he decided to to sneak up quietly, hoping to get close enough to find out more.

"Who is that? I don't remember inviting anybody over?"

As Steve approached the house, he could hear somebody crying. "That's odd." he thought to himself. "Who out here can cry? Zombies moan, skeletons make that 'crack' sound, creepers hiss, and endermans purr." When he was finally close enough to peek over the dirt wall surrounding his house, he noticed there

4

was a witch standing there and crying; not

remembering ever hearing a witch cry, Steve

approached with caution. The witch whirled around in

surprise, staring at Steve. Ready to attack should the

witch decide to throw a potion, Steve stared right

back. The witch, however, did something Steve never

would have expected: APOLOGIZE! The witch

apologized for coming over unannounced and startling

Steve.

"Why are you crying?"

After inviting the witch inside for dinner, Steve began

asking the witch some questions. "Why were you

crying? Why didn't you attack me?" With a puzzled

look on his face, the witch answered, "I was crying

because the witches at home thought I was too soft

when it came to attacking zombies and skeletons. So

they picked on me and called me names. After that,

the decided I didn't deserve to be a witch so they

kicked me out. I'm banished." Steve was so surprised,

he was speechless. How could they do that to

somebody? Realizing this was no ordinary witch,

Steve asked the witch what his name was. Stunned,

the witch said "I don't have one. I've always just been

called 'witch'". So Steve said "From now on, your

name is Alex!" Alex's eyes began to tear up as he

realized he had found a friend. Wanting to return the

kindness he had been shown, Alex told Steve to step

outside so he could use his magic for

good.

"WOW Alex, this house is AMAZING!"

Steve looked on in awe as Alex turned the little

mountainside hole into a mansion fit for a king! Alex

also made it daytime so Steve could see what had

been done for him. After seeing the wonderful new

house that Alex had made, Steve was so happy that he

had taken the time to ask a few questions before

judging his new found friend. Now that Steve had

Alex to help with things around the house, Steve asked Alex to make up some potions to keep them healthy so they'd be able to work faster. They no longer had to worry about protecting the house, as Alex has made a magic barrier around it. Alex also loved working with magic and animals, so Steve asked him to make a farm so that they could have fresh milk every day, and meat whenever they needed it. They also planted a garden filled with potatoes, carrots, watermelons, pumpkins, and wheat when they needed them for exploring.

Chapter 2: Exploring the New World, Up and Down

Now that Steve and Alex had the house, farm and garden setup the way they wanted, Steve decided it was time to explore! He explained to Alex what his plans were and that he might be gone for a few days. Steve excitedly told Alex he'd be back as soon as he had filled his backpack with all the coal, iron, gold, redstone and diamonds he could find. So with his backpack of supplies ready, Steve set out to find what the big, wide world had in store for him.

"I'm going exploring now Alex, watch over the house while I'm gone."

After four hours of walking, Steve came upon a small cave entrance in the side of a hill and decided to go in and explore.

"Hmm, this looks like a nice cave to explore!"

After a short time inside the cave, Steve came across some coal and iron. When he saw this, he felt his heart leap! Now he and Alex could have armor that was tough and tools that lasted longer.

"IRON! I've found iron! We can use this to make armor and weapons!"

"I've also got coal! Now we can run the furnaces as long as we need!"

As Steve mined his way through the iron and coal, he couldn't shake the feeling that he was being watched by somebody or something, so he decided to keep an eye out as he went deeper and deeper into the mineshaft. After taking a short break from mining, he went back to grab his tools, and discovered one was missing. "Odd. I'd swear I put the pickax right next to the sword..." he thought. Shrugging, he brushed it off and continued digging until he fell down a hole and suddenly found himself inside an underground cavern. As he walked around to investigate, he came across some gold! Immediately he went to mine it, but then he heard a noise. Feeling a sense of unease, he decided to wait a second and find out what that noise was. As he started back down the way he had come, he heard the noise again. This time, however, it was much clearer. It was the sound of an arrow whizzing through the air towards him! As he looked around for the archer, what he saw made his heart drop in terror.

"GOLD! ...What was that noise?"

Zombies and skeleton archers were coming at him

from every direction! Their only goal? To turn him

into one of them. As he turned to run back up the path,

he caught a glimpse of a lone creeper wandering

around. This gave him an idea. "I can use the creeper

to kill the zombies following me. Then I can hide

behind this wall, so that the archers have to get closer

and then.... I can attack!" Putting his plan into motion,

he ran towards the creeper... only to realize that there were three more creepers behind it! Not knowing what to do now, he began to dig into the caverns wall so he could try escape what would surely be his death. As he was digging, he heard a familiar sound out in the distance. It was Alex! He was yelling and throwing potions at the attackers. Alex had finished his work at home and decided to follow Steve into the mineshaft. Using the potions, Alex fought off the skeletons, zombies and creepers so that they couldn't get to his friend.

"RUN STEVE! Get back you zombies!"

Seeing Alex bravely battling for him, Steve felt

a new sense of hope. He grabbed his sword and rushed

to Alex's side to battle their enemies head on.

Everything was going well until a stray arrow hit Alex

in the leg. Upon seeing this, Kenclaw felt rage

building up inside of him like he had never felt before.

Taking the opening, Steve began swinging his sword

with renewed strength. After defeating the monsters in

18

front of them, Steve pulled Alex into a small opening in the cavern wall and waited impatiently for the skeleton archer to make his next move. Alex reached out, grasping Steve's hand. "Go! Continue on your journey. I promise, we will meet again." Then with a flash of green light, Alex was gone. Not fully understanding what had just happened to Alex, Steve did what he had told him; Continue on his journey. Steve reached down picked up a bow and arrow from a skeleton archer that he and Alex had defeated and marched back to collect the gold that he and his friend had defended.

"Now I can take this gold. Thank you Alex"

While collecting the gold, Steve still felt like he was being watched. Thinking it was nothing, he continued collecting the gold. As he finished he noticed something flash out of the corner of his eye. Could it be? Had he been wrong and there were even more monsters coming to attack? NO! He had he found the one thing he wanted more than anything else!

"DIAMONDS!" Steve shouted.

Iron Pickaxe

"DIAMONDS!!"

He was so excited to find the diamonds, he forgot

what he had just gone through. "Alex will be so happy

to have these for his magic!" Then it hit him. Alex

was gone. To save Steve, Alex had sacrificed himself.

Chapter 3: Returning Home to a BIG Surprise

It was with a heavy heart that Steve finished collecting everything and started his return journey home. His friend was gone. As he made his way home, he noticed a large group of witches outside his house. Remembering that not all witches were like Alex, Steve approached with caution. As he drew closer, he heard the witches whispering and talking amongst themselves. He was able to make out that they were discussing someone who was missing .

He realized the witches had to be talking about Alex.

Steve carefully made his way through the group.

While he was passing an older looking witch, He felt

someone grab his arm. Ready for anything, Steve

stood firm, waiting to see what was going to happen.

When he heard the crowd gasping and saw them

spread apart, he knew it had to mean something big.

Steve turned, hoping that a miracle had happened and

that Alex would be standing there. He was sad and

disappointed to see it was just the older witch he had passed who had him by the arm. As the witch drew near, Steve noticed there were tears in her eyes, and she spoke with such a quiet voice he barely made out her question. "Do you know where my son is?" Shocked, Steve realized this witch must be Alex's mother. Sighing, he replied "Ma'am, I'm sorry to have to tell you this. He sacrificed himself to save me." Alex's mother began to weep. Suddenly, with no warning, Steve's house started to shake and the ground began to rumble. Even with all the noises surrounding him, Steve could make out a very familiar voice. Alex was standing on top the house, recreating the magical barrier for protection! As soon as Steve saw Alex, he pointed him out to the old witch. The witch cried out

to Alex. Recognizing the voice, Alex ran down to her,

where she was waiting with open arms to give him a

hug. Upon seeing this, everyone began shouting for

joy. Steve decided it was time to put what he had

gathered to good use; A feast in Alex's honor! All of

the witches were invited to join in and Alex was

overjoyed to be reunited with his family. After some

time had passed, Steve pulled Alex aside and said "I

think we're going to need a bigger house!" Hearing

this, Alex burst out laughing and crying at the same

time, realizing that Steve was inviting all the witches

to live with them. Steve, Alex and all the witches

partied through the entire night and into the next

morning.

Steve Discovers a New Land

Chapter 4: The Queen of the Sea

After a few uneventful weeks, Steve decided it was time to go out on an adventure again. Saying goodbye to Alex and all of his new friends, Steve packed up again and started off to explore. Not wanting him to have to walk the entire way, the witches made him a special boat. Steve climbed into the boat and cast off for new lands to explore. Shortly after he'd begun his journey, a big storm rolled through, causing him to get knocked off course. Lost at sea, Steve decided to pick a direction and start rowing, hoping for the best. After he'd been rowing for some time, he started to hear a voice, singing. "Oh come, oh come all ye sailors to me! For I am the ruler and queen of the sea. If you wish to test my depths, you will need to pass my test. If you desire to cross my sea, a special gift you must bring to me!" Steve was trying to figure out where the voice was coming from.

"Where is that singing coming from? And why are there lights down there?"

When suddenly a mermaid rose out of the water right next to his ship! Startled, Steve asked "Who are you!?" "I am the queen of the sea" she answered. After a pause, Steve said "Well, it was nice meeting you, Queen of the Sea. But would you look at that sun? I really must be going now..." "Not so fast!" the mermaid shouted, grabbing on to his boat with a tight grip. "What do you want with me?" Steve asked, nervously. "If you wish to cross me sea, a special gift you must bring to me! Didn't you hear my song?" she said with exasperation. "What gift?" Steve asked her. "You must bring me five diamonds from the cave of Shimmering Pools." she said. "FIVE DIAMONDS!?" Steve shouted. *"This isn't such a good deal...."* he thought to himself. He began to try and think of a way out of it. *"I've got it!"* He said to himself. To the mermaid he said "But why would you make me swim all the way down there?? My house has tons of diamonds in it." "WHAT!? Tons of diamonds you say? Hm... Well. Then I will take you safely across the sea in return for half of your diamonds!" *"I've got her!"* Steve thought, *"Now all I have to do is make it to a place on land where I can run away!"* However all of his plans were useless. When they arrived to shore, the mermaid said "Now! Tell me where the diamonds are. I'll send my men to collect them and once they've returned, you can go."

This was definitely not going the way Steve had hoped it would. When the Queen said she would send men to collect the diamonds, he knew he had to come up with something that would keep her men busy for a while so that he could escape. So Steve drew them a map that went all over the place. Over mountains, through rivers, inside caves and over forests. With the map finished, the Queen's men set out to find the diamond house, not realizing they had been duped.

Unable to think of anything else but the diamonds she

was about to have, the Queen began to loosen her grip

on Steve's boat. Seeing that she was distracted, Steve

slowly began moving his boat closer to shore in an

effort to make his escape. When he was just about to

make his escape, the Queen's men returned with the

diamonds. "Here they are, my queen!" said one of the

men.*"Where did they get those from?"* Steve

thought. **Boom! Boom! Boom! Boom!**the ground

began shaking and the water started moving like a

mighty wind was blowing over the surface. "Who

DARES to take MY diamonds!?!?" yelled a loud,

deep voice. "Where did you get those from?" the

Queen asked her men. Not knowing what to do, and not wanting to stick around to find out where the diamonds came from, Steve jumped from his boat and began to run to the woods nearby for cover. What he saw coming towards him, however, made him stop in his tracks. There, towering over the trees, was a GIANT!

"A GIANT?!?! IN MINECRAFT?!?"

A giant... Indeed, the Queen's men had stolen the diamonds from the Giant of the island. Summoning everything he had in him, Steve ran to the forest and tried to find somewhere to hide from the giant. But hiding was useless. How do you hide from something taller than the trees?

"Ok he didn't notice me so now I need to hide, QUICK!"

After the giant had lumbered past, Steve began to frantically look for a cave or a small hole near a tree to hide in. When he spotted the way a certain tree was growing, he decided to use the tree to hide in. No one would think to look inside a tree! So Steve snuck over to the tree, trying not to attract the giant's attention. Looking inside, he decided the tree would make a great house, so he began to work at converting the tree into his new home. He added some glowstone for light and wooden blocks to keep the leaves from going away. Then Steve added a big chest, furnace, and a crafting table so he could build, smelt, cook and store all the food he would find. After getting his new home set up and running, Steve started to explore. He remained wary of the Giant still walking around, though.

"There, all done and it looks great!"

"WOW! That house is HUGE!"

Chapter 5. The Giants House

While exploring, Steve came across something amazing.... The Giant's house!! The house was incredible! it had so much stuff inside. Stuff that Steve could use for all sorts of things, but Steve was cautious not to take too much. If the Giant were to discover things missing, he would surely come after Steve and want all of his stuff back.

"Wow, he even has iron golems protecting his house?"

Steve couldn't believe his eyes when he saw everything there was!

"WOAH!!!! LOOK AT ALL THE DIAMOND!?"

After taking all the diamonds he could hold, he

decided to head back to his new tree-house and store it

away for safekeeping. As Steve was leaving the

house, he head the one thing he didn't want to

hear...... **THUMP, THUMP, THUMP,**

THUMP! The giant had returned home after

reclaiming his diamonds from the Queen of the Sea. As the Giant approached his house he realized something wasn't right and began to look around to find what was wrong. After looking around a bit, the Giant finally found what was wrong. As Steve stood motionless in his hiding spot, he couldn't shake the feeling that he needed to run as fast as he could. However, knowing the Giant would most definitely catch him, Steve decided to stay. As the Giant moved forward, following the new smell he had discovered, Steve decided it was time to run! He took off as fast as he could without bothering to look back. Steve ran out the door, up the hill, and swam across the small lake. When he stopped to rest and see where he was, what he saw in front of him filled him with even more fear.

"I'm in big trouble....a Giant village?? Are you kidding me???"

It was a village of Giants!! Running around the

houses, he noticed a bowl shape in the middle of the

village. Deciding this may be the perfect spot to hide,

Steve made a dash towards it.

"The Giants have a village in their village?"

As he drew closer, he realized what it was he saw, a village that looked as if it had risen out of the sea. While trying to make sense out of what he was looking at, Steve heard the sound again. **THUMP, THUMP, THUMP, THUMP!** "Where are you, you little thief!?" Steve heard the Giant yell. So Steve got up and started running again. Through another lake, another forest, over another mountain. When heard the

final **THUMP** he knew he was in

trouble.

"There you are you THIEF!!"

Steve wasn't sure what to do. Should he try to run and

hide in the forest? Should he try to dig into the

mountain? Nothing he could think of was going to

work. *"If I hide in the forest, he'll rip the trees out of*

the ground. If I hide in the mountain, he'll break it

down with his bare hands." Suddenly, Steve felt

himself being picked up off the ground and carried through the air. He squeezed his eyes shut. After the moving stopped, Steve decided to take a look to see where he was. And what he saw struck fear into him like he'd never felt before. Steve was face to face with THE GIANT!

"Why were you taking my diamonds little thief?!!"

Steve couldn't help but feel a massive amount of fear swelling up inside him. "Why are you taking my diamonds? And why were you leading that Sea Witch and her men to my house!?" Steve began to explain that the Queen had him in the middle of the ocean, so he made up a house with diamonds to get her near shore so he could escape, and that when the men had returned with ACTUAL diamonds, he knew there was going to be trouble. As the Giant listened to Steve's story, he couldn't help but laugh at the end. "HAHAHAHAHAHA!!! You actually thought that Sea Witch would keep her end of a bargain?" Not fully understanding what the Giant meant, Steve asked him to explain. "Can you please tell me why you keep calling her the'Sea Witch'? I thought she was the Queen of the Sea?" The Giant said "First, allow me to introduce myself. I am Borgron the Brave, King of what was once the mightiest city in all of Hazgorn... Feridon!" Then Borgron told Steve all sorts of wonderful stories about the time before the Sea Demons had arrived. "One day we were having our yearly celebration in honor of the newest soldiers in our army. As we were toasting them to many victories, the ground began to rumble. Houses started to shake. Then, without any warning, the middle of the city split open into a small village rising from the depths of the sea. As it reached the surface, Sea Demons started attacking from everywhere. They used magic, spears, bows, swords... all manner of weapons. We were defenseless against the sudden assault and were forced to abandon our beloved city. I stayed

behind with my closest and most trusted soldiers to

protect the villagers from attacks. By the time we had

completely evacuated the city and pulled back, there

were only 7 of us remaining from the 30 who had

stood firm." Borgron's gaze drifted off to space as he

was remembering the friends he had lost that day.

"Ever since then, I have made it my sole duty to rid

Hazgorn of the Sea Demons for good!" Steve began to

look at Borgron in a different light. Borgron wasn't

this mean giant, out to get everyone. Borgron was a

King who had lost everything and wanted to make

sure it didn't happen to anyone else ever again. "If

you're afraid the Sea Demons will attack again, why

do you live so close to the ocean where they attack from?" Understanding Steve's confusion, Borgron explained, "If I do not live here and keep them from attacking others, then who will?" Steve saw the giant in a different way after that. He wasn't some terrible monster like he had thought; he was someone willing to stand alone against the Sea Queen and her army to protect everybody in Hazgorn. "They attacked us and drove us from our homes. I have been trying to find their base so I can drive them back into the sea, but I haven't been able to find it for some reason. They must be hiding it with some sort of powerful magic." Borgron explained. Steve now knew then what he had to do. He had badly misjudged the Giants and had even tried to steal from them! He was going to find a way to make it up to them and help them get their home back. Steve was going on an adventure like he had never been on before: He was going to find the Sea Demon's base and help the Giants take back their home!

"I wonder where the Sea Demons could be hiding

After looking around here and there, Steve couldn't find any sort of base. As he searched, he found a garden filled with watermelons, carrots, potatoes,

wheat, and even pumpkins! There was a fence around

it so Steve thought there must be somebody that takes

care of it, but who?

"That's a nice garden, but why would people from the sea eat land food?"

After walking around the garden and doing some

more looking, he decided to move further down the

coast. After a day of searching, he was returning to

Borgron to ask some questions about where he thought the base might be, when he saw something glowing in the distance. Steve decided to find out what it was. He spent all of the day, and most of the night, searching for it. At last he found what he was looking for. The base of the Sea Demons was sitting right there near the shore, but there was something odd about it. *"I know I walked past this before... the base wasn't here then.."* After looking closer, Steve figured it out. "THAT'S IT!" he shouted. "It can only be seen at night! THAT'S why Borgron hasn't found it yet!"

"Now I can go back and tell Borgron some good news!"

Excited to share the news, Steve hurried back to Borgron. As he neared Borgron's house, he noticed something odd; the door was open. Walking inside, Steve found the golems lying motionless on the ground, and the house was a total wreck. Steve looked around, puzzled. "What could've attacked Borgron AND his iron golems?" he muttered to himself. Looking around for clues, he soon found his answer. *"AHA!"* he said. *"Magic burns on the walls and water tracks on the floor... This can only mean one thing...."* "THE SEA DEMONS HAVE TAKEN HIM!!"

"That's a lot of witches, but Borgron is in there and I'm going to get him out!"

Steve shouted. Now that Steve knew where they had taken him, he just had to figure out a plan to get him back. Before Steve could really think of anything, he heard the sound of a shell horn blowing in the

distance; the Sea Witch was taking her victim down to

the blue depths below. Out of time and completely

outnumbered, Steve had but one choice: ATTACK!

As Steve charged down the hill yelling and swinging

his sword, the Sea Demons were confused. They

weren't sure what they were seeing.... A lone human

was charging their army? To save a giant? "Kill him!"

hissed the Sea Queen. "BORGRON!!! I'M

COMING!!!!" Steve shouted as he reached the beach.

Hearing his small friend rushing in to save him,

Borgron felt his strength return, like a wave crashing

over him. Reaching down to pick up his sword,

Borgron cut the ropes holding his legs together.

Seeing that the Giant had gotten loose and realizing how dangerous he was, the Sea Demons started to scatter in all different directions, afraid to face the Giant King's wrath. King Borgron let out a mighty battle cry, and then something happened that took Steve by surprise. The ground began to shake, then the army of Feridon came in with full force to aid their king. Steve looked on in awe as the army of giants ran over him to battle the Sea Demons away and reclaim their home!

"Thanks for the diamonds Borgron but I must be moving on."

Chapter 6. Iron Golem Vorg

Now that King Borgron was safe and seeing the kingdom of Feridon returning to normal, Steve decided it was time to move on. He had more exploring to do. Borgron refused to let Steve leave empty-handed. "Return here when you are finished exploring. When you are ready to return home, I will give you a ship and a crew to escort you safely across the sea. Don't think I will forget to reward you for saving me and giving us the courage to fight for our land." Borgron said as he personally escorted Steve to the edge of the kingdom. After saying their goodbyes, Steve began walking north. Just as he started to disappear from sight, Borgron shouted out "Make sure to keep an eye out for golems! There is said to be a

certain one that can use his eyes to turn you into

stone!" Making a note of this, Steve continued on his

journey to explore the world and find the perfect place

to set up the house where he would live forever.

"Oh no there's an iron golem trapped in the ground!"

Soon, Steve spotted a hole in the ground. In order to

get a better look, he climbed a tree. Looking down

into the hole, he was shocked by what he saw. An iron

golem was trapped!

"Don't worry! I'm going to get you out of there!"

Momentarily forgetting Borgron's warning, Steve rushed over to help the golem escape by filling the hole with dirt and water. After working for hours, Steve was successful! The golem was freed!

"There you go, you're free now."

As the golem finished making his way out of the hole,

Steve recalled Borgron's words. *"Make sure to keep*

an eye out for golems. There is said to be one that

uses his eyes to turn you to stone." Steve tried to back

slowly away from the golem, in hopes of putting some

space between them so he wouldn't be turned to stone.

As he backed away, however, the golem moved

forward.

It doesn't look good for Steve.

Turning to run, Steve noticed a pain in his feet, so he

glanced down while running to see what was wrong.

HE WAS BEING TURNED INTO STONE!!! Steve

stumbled while trying to run. Looking down, he

watched as his body was being turned into stone. The

golem approached him and started dragging him

towards a strange looking castle in the distance. Steve

had no idea who or what lived there, but he knew it

wasn't going to be good. All Steve could do was

watch as they neared what he thought must be Golem

Castle.

Steve as right, the golem was taking him to their castle!

Now that the golems had him, Steve wasn't sure what

to do. Could he try to escape? He started to think, but

when your body is made of stone, it's pretty hard to

run or move. *"I know!"* he thought. *"I could trick the*

golems into turning me back to normal!" But after

thinking about it, he realized that wouldn't work either. He was in a real pickle this time, and he couldn't think of a way to get out. Then a voice thundered out of nowhere. "Store him in the castle for now. The Sea Queen will be here later to take him and pay us." Then the voice turned to Steve. "Now what is it that you could've done that would make the Sea Queen so angry she would seek my help?" Steve decided he'd better choose his words carefully. He needed to try and find out as much as he could about who this golem was. "First, who are you?" he addressed the golem. "ME?? YOU DON'T KNOW WHO I AM!?" thundered the golem. "I am Vorg, King of the Iron Golem Clan! Mightiest warrior who ever lived!" Steve was puzzled. He thought this golem would be more of a silent golem and use magic, but warriors don't typically use magic, they use swords and bows. "I was told that there lived an iron golem near here who used magic to turn you into stone and make you serve him. Is that you?" Steve asked. Vorg looked puzzled, then burst into laughter.

"HAHAHAHA!" Goodness no. People see us use our stone gaze to capture our enemies and think that means we turn them into golems!? Pfft. Humans are not worthy of becoming part of the Iron Golem race!" Now Steve understood what Borgron had meant. It wasn't a magic using golem that he had been warning Steve about. Golems used their stone gaze to capture people. THAT is what he meant.

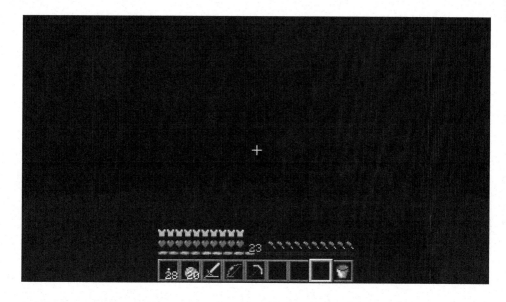

"This castle is our only refuge here since the Sea Queen arrived in Hazgorn"

After Vorg explained how the golems had lost their homes when the giants had been defeated, Steve decided to tell him that the Sea Queen had been defeated and the giants had reclaimed their homes. "If the Sea Queen and her people did this, then I have great news for you!" Steve said. Vorg froze in his tracks, hoping that Steve was about to tell him the one thing he'd been waiting to hear for a long time. "King Borgron was captured by the Queen.." "WHAT!?" Vorg interrupted. "How is that good news!? If Borgron has been captured, then there is no hope for winning this war!" Vorg cried. Steve continued, "He was captured by them, yes, but I ran in to save him. Borgron's strength returned, and he was able to pick up his sword once again! With a mighty cry, the army of Feridon charged down the beaches and attacked the Queen and her demons. After hearing this Vorg uses his stone gaze to reverse the spell on Steve and put him back to normal. Vorg's eyes changed from being almost black to a bright red. He ran out of the castle and into the courtyard where the golems were standing. "BORGRON AND HIS ARMY HAVE DONE IT!! THAT SEA WITCH HAS BEEN DEFEATED!!!" Vorg yelled throughout the entire castle. The Iron Golem Clan began to shout for joy, and some of them commenced singing. Vorg took Steve aside and asked him to accompany him back to Feridon and introduce him to King Borgron. "I would be happy to, but you see, I am on my way out to explore more of the world. I need to find a place to build my 'forever' house." Vorg interrupted him again, explaining, "You don't understand. We golems have portals set up around the world. We can teleport back and forth at will." Vorg then showed him the pools of teleportation. "The one on your left leads to our homeland underground, Draunforge. The one there on your right leads to Feridon. And the center pool there, that's the one we'll reappear here in." Steve was amazed at the abilities of the Iron Golems and agreed to accompany Vorg to Feridon.

"This is amazing! These pools will teleport you home or to Feridon?"

Steve watched in amazement as the golems jumped

into the pool one by one and disappeared. When it came his turn, King Vorg said "Don't be afraid! Just jump right in!" So Steve smiled and jumped into the pool. Before he could even blink, he was standing in the center of Feridon where the giants were rebuilding the city, an effort to return it to its former glory. The giants were puzzled by the sudden appearance of the Iron Golem Clan, so they sent for King Borgron. When Borgron arrived, he felt very displeased that the golems felt comfortable enough to just appear in the center of his city without warning, until there in the middle of the group, Steve appeared. Steve was standing next to the Iron Golem King, King Vorg. Vorg looked up at Borgron and said "Oh great King

Borgron! I heard tell from this little human that you have defeated the Sea Queen and banished her back to the depths! Is this true?" Seeing that Steve hadn't heeded his warning, Borgron couldn't help but laugh. "Hahahaha! It seems that yet again you have put yourself in a sticky situation, haven't you Steve?" Steve couldn't help it. He laughed too. "Well, you know me Borgron. Going to mess it up every time!" Vorg then offered Borgron the aid of the Iron Golem Clan in rebuilding the city, as a gift for having defeated the Sea Queen.

Deep in the depths of the sea, the Sea Witch sat, stewing. Even though she'd been defeated, she hadn't forgotten who the cause of her problems was. "Steve!! You will pay for thissss! You will pay for EVERYTHING!" she hissed. "GUARDS! I want you to send out our best spies and find me Steve..... NOW!"

Chapter 7. Into the Jungle

Having portaled back to the Iron Golem's castle, and being gifted with food and weapons, he was now set out to explore more of the world. After 7days of walking he found a jungle and decided to do some exploring in there, so he climbed a very tall tree and made a base. After he finished building he decided to take a look at his view.

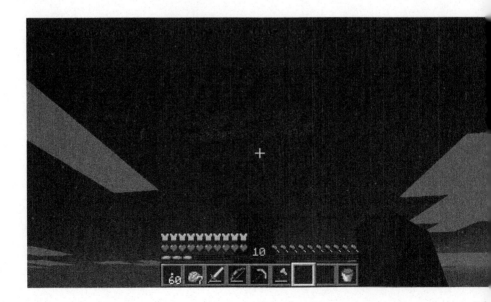

"It looks good. Gotta keep it hidden so people can't find it"

After Looking at the house and checking around he went inside to fix it up a bit and make it a home.

"Now I just have to fix it up a bit and Im done!"

While he was working inside he heard noise outside the door, like somebody trying to listen. "Stop moving around he is going to hear us." The spies from the Sea Queen whispered. "Hmm. I wonder what that noise was?" Steve asked himself. As he moved towards the

door the two spies ran towards the lake near his house.

Steve opened the door and looked around to see if

someone was there. Not seeing any signs of anybody

being there, he turned around to go back inside but

noticed something out of the corner of his eye.

"I wonder what that is in the lake?"

Not sure what he was seeing, Steve moved in to get a

closer look at the building. As he got closer it slowly

took shape. Closer and closer he moved until he could

see the torches on the outside. "What is that? Could It

be a temple maybe?" He thought to himself. Deciding

the only way to find out was to go have a look for

himself, Steve climbed down.

"That's what it is alright, a Jungle Temple!"

Steve moved in closer to do some exploring inside and

see what treasures the temple had within. As he got

closer he realized something he hadn't noticed from a

distance. "OH NO! The temple is full of skeletons and zombies!" Henlcaw hadn't noticed the amount of zombies and skeletons from far away and now he was going to have to fight his way inside the temple. Pulling out his bow, Steve prepared to fight.

"TAKE THIS ZOMBIE! HA FIRE IN THE FACE!"

As he shot arrow after arrow, Steve could see no end to the zombies. After what seemed like hours of fighting he finally saw the end in sight, getting every bit of strength he had left in him and charged the

remaining skeleton archers. Cutting his way through

the zombies that remained in front of the temple,

Steve climbed the cobblestone steps and walked inside

and as he did an arrow whizzed past his face. He

turned to face the skeleton and charged. "HERE I

COME YOU BONEY PIECE OF JUNK!" He cried as

he ran in swinging his sword. Finally reaching the

bottom floor and killing all the skeletons Steve saw

the temple chest.

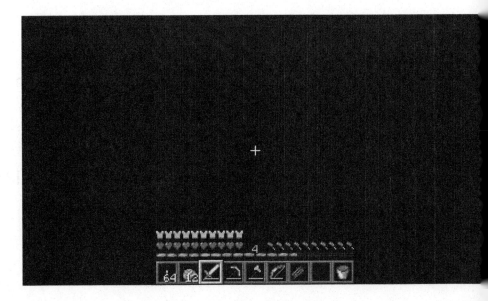

"AHA! There it is just waiting for me!"

He ran over to open the chest and see what treasure it

held and was not let down. When he opened it the

chest contained gold, iron, and diamonds!

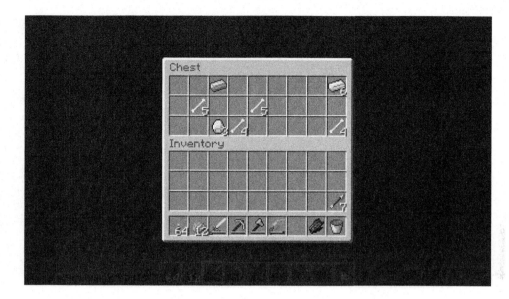

"YES! I FOUND MORE DIAMONDS!"

When he had finished collecting everything, Steve

went outside to head home. As he was about to jump

into the lake he noticed something in the trees.

"Who is that?"

As he tried to get closer to whomever it was,

something happened that he didn't expect. The two

witches vanished into thin air then lava and water

started flowing from the tops of the trees they had

been sitting in.

"WHAT?? WHAT IN THE WORLD JUST HAPPENED?!"

As Steve watched, lava flowed down the trees followed by water. He decided it was time to go home and turned around and ran. When he got home he noticed a strange light coming from his roof and so he rushed inside to see what it was. When he got inside his jaw dropped at what he saw. "Lava in my house??? Who would do this to me?!?!" Lava indeed.

The Queens spies had decided to troll him while he was away so they poured lava in his house.

"WHY WOULD THEY DO THIS????"

Steve paced back and forth outside as lava burned down his house and all the stuff from Vorg and Borgron. "Who would do this? WHO WOULD DO THIS?" He asked himself over and over again. Then an even scarier question came to him... "Who is out here other than me that COULD do this?" That was a scary question indeed. As he paced back and forth

thinking, something moved behind him. He grabbed

his sword and stood ready to attack. When the two

spies revealed themselves Steve was puzzled at first.

"Who are you two?" He asked.

"We were sent by the Queen to capture you."

After realizing these men were from the Sea Queen,

Henlcaw tried to run but they had already poisoned

him with a potion that made him sleepy. After

capturing him, the two spies used their magic to

teleport back to the Queen to give her Steve. "YOUR

MAJESTY!!! We have him!! We have Steve!!" they

shouted as they ran towards the throne room.

"Wonderful! Wonderful! Steve at last iissssss

miiiine!" The Queen hissed. "Now you will pay for

what you did to us in Feridon, Steve!" "Take him to

the dungeon!" So the guards picked him up by his

arms and dragged him out of the room.

"Welcome to my kingdom Steve. You won't be leaving anytime soon!"

Chapter 8. Steves Sticky Situation

Far away on the other side of the world, Alex felt something was wrong with Steve. He had used his magic on him so he could tell whenever he was in trouble.

Alex gathers the witches to save Steve

Alex tells all the witches that Steve is in danger and they need to save him. The witches combine their magic and teleport to Feridon. Borgron and Vorg were

finishing their goodbyes when in the center of the

town square a portal opened. Both kings immediately

had their armies ready for another Sea Demon

invasion attempt. The Iron Golems stood ready to use

their stone gaze on the Demons and the giants held

their swords and axes close. Out of the portal popped

Alex and the witches. Stunned by the army in front of

them Alex asked. "Where is Steve!?" Vorg looked at

Borgron in puzzlement and said. "Could this be the

witch that he spoke of from home?" Borgron thought

back to Steves description of Alex and finally said.

"You must be Alex then. Why do you seek Steve?"

Alex explained how he had used his magic on him and

that he felt Steve was in danger under the sea or

somewhere dark. Hearing 'under the sea' Borgron and

Vorg looked at each other with complete shock.

"Feridons Steve is in trouble and needs our help. To the depths of the sea!"

Feridons! We march on the Sea Queens capital of

Alamtas! Borgron shouted. Vorg also readied his

golems for battle.

"Steve helped rid us of the Sea Queen on our shores and now he needs us!"

Alex and the witches finished making their potions

and magic shields for the giants to be able to breathe

under water. After all the preparations were finished

Alex and the witches, Borgron and the giants, and

Vorg with his Iron Golems marched towards the sea.

Alex summoned an army of skeleton archers and

ghasts to aid them in battle.

"You ghasts and skeletons will aid me in battle!"

On the Beach Alex commanded the ghasts and

skeletons to dive into the depths and lay siege to

Alamta's gates. Borgron and Vorg took their armies to

the rear of the city to burst through the unguarded

gates and charge the castle.

The gates of Alamtas

As Alexs forces arrived at the gates, the army of Alamtas marched out. The ghasts let loose the explosive shots and the archers released arrow after arrow. Alex and the witches began bombarding them with potions and magic from behind the skeletons. Alex shot off the signal potion to tell Borgron and Vorg to charge.

"FERIDONS! TO WAAAAAAAAAAAAAAAR!"

Borgron saw the potion and ordered the giants and

golems out of hiding and into battle! Borgron rammed

the gate with his hammer and put all his might behind

it. The gate burst open and the combined armies of

Hazgorn poured into Alamtas and marched on the

Queen's castle.

"There is the castle gate! Follow me!!!"

Borgron led the army of Feridon though the courtyard

and into the castle. Vorg and the Iron Golems went

straight through the royal guards with their stone stare

and down to the dungeons to rescue Steve! Borgron

and the giants kept the guards and Queen at bay while

Vorg and the golems went for Steve. The Sea Queen,

enraged by the attack, used all her magical ability

against them. One of her spells hit Borgron in the

heart and brought him down. The giants, seeing their

leader go down, fought not only to save Steve, but

now to protect their leader!

"Yesssssssss Borgron the mighty has fallen. Attack NOW!"

As the Queen's forces began another attack on the

retreating giants, through the gates burst Alex and the

witches for a second attack. The Sea Queen couldn't

believe what she was seeing and retreated inside her

of chambers. Alex ordered two witches to heal

Borgron and anybody else that had been injured. After

they finished, Borgron jumped up and charged after

the Queen. Borgron caught up to the queen and

grabbed her and picked her up.

"YOU ARE DONE SEA QUEEN!"

The Sea Queen couldn't escape Borgrons grip. As

Borgron carried her out of the castle, the combined

armies were finishing the only guards left. As Alex's

witches finished healing everybody that had been

injured, Steve came up from the dungeons with Vorg

and his golems. Steve was amazed that all of his

friends had come together to rescue him.

Chapter 9. Steve Settles Down

After returning to Feridon, Alex and the Iron Golems create a magic stone prison cell that will keep the Queen sealed away for the rest of time. "There she shall remain, trapped in her stone prison in the dungeons of Feridon." Borgron said. "Guarded by a combined force of Golems and Giants, there she will be till the end of time." Said Vorg, stepping forward.

"LET THE PARTY BEGIN!!"

Then Borgron begins shooting off fireworks to signal

the beginning of the all night party! Steve, Alex,

Vorg, and Borgron sit around a table sharing stories of

all the adventures they had been on with each other

and tales of great battles before. After the story telling,

Borgron gets up and walks to the top of the hill

overlooking the city and started singing and dancing.

Shortly after he began, all the giants covered the

hilltop and were singing and dancing all night!

"Look at Borgron go, Alex!"

Alex and Steve joined in with the giants and partied

all night long. Meanwhile, Vorg and the golems were

creating statues and fountains for   Feridon. Vorg

pulled Steve aside and thanked him for everything he

had done to help the Iron Golems.

"Thank you Steve, for everything."

After talking to Vorg, Borgron asked to speak to Steve in private.

"You have done so much for all of us Steve."

"Steve, thank you for taking the time and getting to know me."

Alex and Steve stood on the wall and watched the

show as the sun set. Steve decided this was a place he

could live happily, surrounded by friends.

CPSIA information can be obtained
at www.ICGtesting.com
Printed in the USA
LVOW04s1107251116

514436LV00012B/486/P